Life Around the World
Clothes in Many Cultures

Heather Adamson

Raintree is an imprint of Capstone Global Library Limited, a company incorporated in England and Wales having its registered office at 264 Banbury Road, Oxford, OX2 7DY – Registered company number: 6695582

www.raintree.co.uk
myorders@raintree.co.uk

Edited by Sarah L Schuette
Designed by Alison Thiele
Picture research by Kara Birr
Originated by Capstone Global Library Ltd
Printed and bound in India

ISBN 978 1 4747 3534 6 (hardback)
20 19 18 17 16
10 9 8 7 6 5 4 3 2 1

ISBN 978 1 4747 3539 1 paperback)
21 20 19 18 17
10 9 8 7 6 5 4 3 2 1

British Library Cataloguing in Publication Data
A full catalogue record for this book is available from the British Library.

Acknowledgements

Capstone Press: Design Element (map); Getty Images: Michael Sewell, 7; iStockphoto: andresr, 5; Shutterstock: Dario Diament, 1, Elena Elisseeva, 20, Geir Olav Lyngfjell, 9, Inna Tyshchenko, 15, JT Lewis, 19, leungchopan, 11, Lincoln Rogers, 17, Suriya99, Cover; Thinkstock: Anne Greenwood, 13

Every effort has been made to contact copyright holders of material reproduced in this book. Any omissions will be rectified in subsequent printings if notice is given to the publisher.

All the Internet addresses (URLs) given in this book were valid at the time of going to press. However, due to the dynamic nature of the Internet, some addresses may have changed, or sites may have changed or ceased to exist since publication. While the author and publisher regret any inconvenience this may cause readers, no responsibility for any such changes can be accepted by either the author or the publisher.

Contents

Clothes to wear 4

Work clothes 10

Traditional clothes 14

Your clothes 20

Glossary 22

Find out more 23

Websites 23

Index 24

Clothes to wear

Around the world,
everyone wears clothes
for work or play.

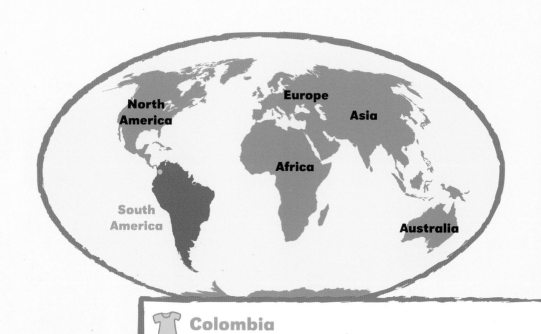

North America

Europe

Asia

Africa

South America

Australia

👕 Colombia

Parkas keep people warm
on cold days.

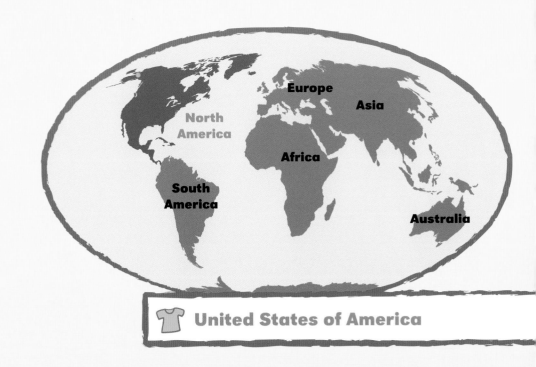

North
America

Europe

Asia

Africa

South
America

Australia

👕 United States of America

Sarongs keep people cool
on hot days.

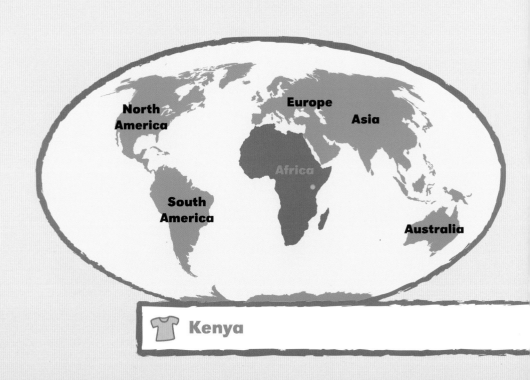

Kenya

Work clothes

Office workers wear business suits to their jobs.

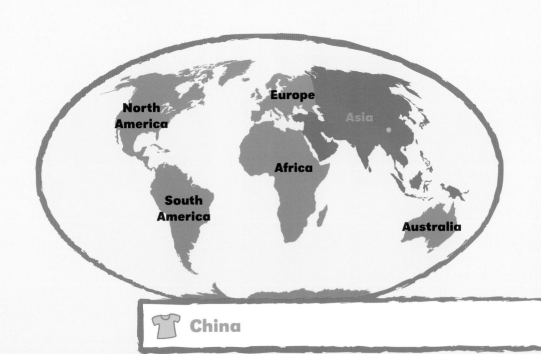

North America

Europe

Asia

Africa

South America

Australia

China

Ranchers wear sturdy jeans
when they work outside.

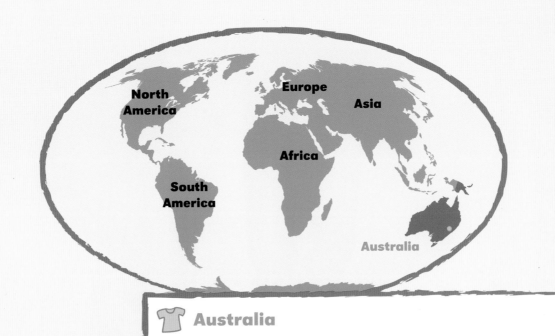

North America

Europe

Asia

Africa

South America

Australia

👕 Australia

Traditional clothes

Brides and grooms wear
fancy clothes
on their wedding day.

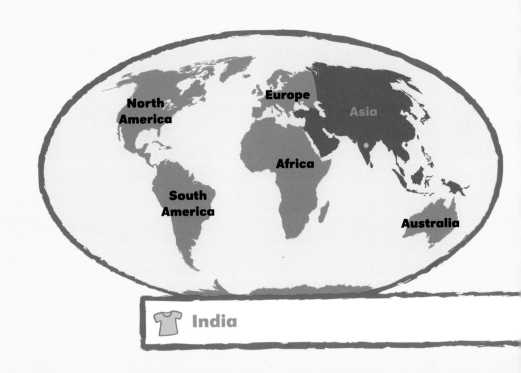

North America

Europe

Asia

Africa

South America

Australia

👕 India

Native Americans wear bright colors to dance at powwows.

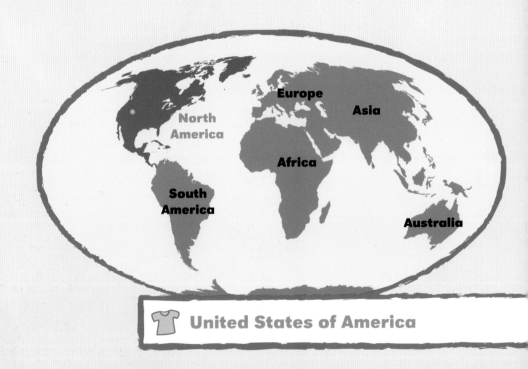

United States of America

Scottish men wear
kilts in parades
and at ceremonies.

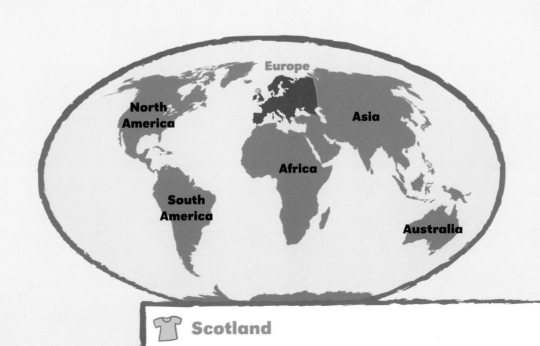

Europe

North
America

Asia

Africa

South
America

Australia

Scotland

Your clothes

Clothes are different around the world. What did you wear today?

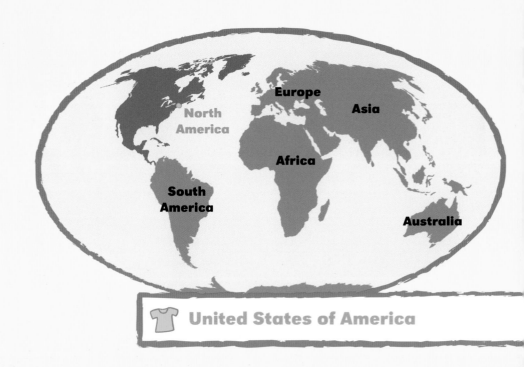

North America

Europe

Asia

Africa

South America

Australia

United States of America

Glossary

bride woman who is about to get married

business suit set of matching clothes that includes a jacket and trousers or a jacket and skirt

ceremony formal actions, words and music performed to mark an important occasion

groom man who is about to get married

kilt tartan skirt with pleats or folds

parka large heavy coat made with fur

powwow social gathering where Native Americans dance, tell stories and celebrate traditions

sarong piece of cloth wrapped around the body

sturdy strong and stiff

Find out more

Clothes Around the World (Around the World), Clare Lewis
(Heinemann Library, 2014)

Clothes Around the World (Children Like Us), Moira Butterfield
(Wayland, 2016)

What We Wear, Maya Ajmera, Elise Hofer Durstine & Cynthia
Pon (Charlesbridge Publishing, 2012)

Websites

http://www.childrensuniversity.manchester.ac.uk/interactives/art&design/
talkingtextiles/costume/
Fun facts about dressing up around the world.

https://www.roughguides.com/gallery/traditional-dress/#/0
Photo gallery of traditional clothing from around the world.

Index

brides   14

business suits   10

ceremonies   18

colorful clothes   16

cool clothes   8

fancy clothing   14

grooms   14

jeans   12

kilts   18

Native Americans   16

office workers   10

parades   18

parkas   6

powwows   16

ranchers   12

sarongs   8

warm clothes   6

work clothing   4, 10, 12